**LifeTimes**

# The Story of
# Martin Luther King

by James Riordan
illustrated by Rob McCaig

Thameside Press

Distributed in the United States by
Smart Apple Media
1980 Lookout Drive
North Mankato, MN 56003

Text copyright © James Riordan 2001

Editor: Steve White-Thomson
Designer: Simon Borrough
Language consultant: Norah Granger, Senior Lecturer
 in Primary Education at the University of Brighton, U.K.
With thanks to Kay Barnham for her editorial help
 in the latter stages of this book.

**Library of Congress Cataloging–in–Publication Data**

Riordan, James, 1936–
   The story of Martin Luther King / written by James Riordan.
      p.  cm.  -- (Lifetimes)
   Includes index.
   ISBN 1-930643-24-1
      1. King, Martin Luther, Jr., 1929–1968--Juvenile literature. 2. African
   Americans--Biography--Juvenile literature. 3. Civil rights workers--United
   States--Biography--Juvenile literature. 4. Baptists--United States--Clergy--
   Biography--Juvenile literature. 5. African Americans--Civil rights--History--
   20th century--Juvenile literature. [1. King, Martin Luther, Jr., 1929–1968.
   2. Civil rights workers. 3. Clergy. 4. African Americans--Biography.] I. Title.
   II. Lifetimes (North Mankato, Minn.)

   E185.97.K5 R57 2001
   323'.092--dc21
   [B]                                                                     2001027273

Printed in Hong Kong

9  8  7  6  5  4  3  2  1

# Introduction

Martin Luther King, Jr. was born on
January 15, 1929, in Atlanta, Georgia. At the
age of 19, Martin became a Baptist minister
like his father and devoted the rest of his life
to preaching God's word and helping the
African-American community.

At that time, black people in the southern
states had few rights. If they tried to protest,
they risked being put in jail. Worse still, they
might be burned or lynched by white people.

In early December 1955, Martin had just
become minister of the Dexter Baptist Church
in Montgomery, Alabama...

# The Seat on the Bus

Her name was Rosa Parks. She lived in
Montgomery, in the state of Alabama.

Her job in a store did not pay much, and
Rosa worked long hours to make ends meet.

One evening after work, Rosa caught the bus as usual. She had been on her feet all day and was exhausted.

It was rush hour, and the bus was almost full. All the seats in the back were taken, so Rosa had to sit in the middle, behind the whites-only seats.

At the next stop, some white people got on. They sat at the front of the bus, but one man had to stand.

The driver looked back at Rosa.

"Give him your seat!" he shouted loudly. In this town it was the law that black people had to give up the middle seats of a bus to white people.

But today Rosa was tired. She didn't feel like giving up her seat.

"No, I won't," she said calmly, before turning to stare out of the window.

"Hey, nigger woman!" cried the driver, getting angry. "You heard me. Give the white man your seat!"

She sighed. Why should she stand for a man just because he was white?

"No, I won't!" Rosa repeated, louder this time.

Other passengers, white and black, glared
at her. She was holding up the whole bus.

"Stand up or I'll call the cops!" warned
the driver.

But, for once, Rosa didn't care. Let the cops
come. She was sick of being pushed around.

Within a few minutes, two policemen had
arrived, and she was on her way to jail.

Much later, Rosa was charged with breaking the city's bus laws.

"I understand," she replied with a sigh. "Now, I've waited a long time, and it's hot. May I have a drink of water, please?" she asked

"No, ours is a whites-only water fountain."

"But it isn't a whites-only phone," she said.

"I can make one phone call." Rosa knew her rights. After all, she'd worked for the local Black Help organization. So she phoned a friend. "Brother," she said, "I'm in jail for sitting on a bus."

Little did she know what she was starting.

For 300 years, millions of black Africans had been taken to America as slaves. In 1865 slavery ended, yet several states in the south refused to give black people equal rights.

When Rosa Parks made her bus protest in 1955, she broke Alabama's segregation laws. The laws gave the best jobs, schools, and restaurants to white people... and the best bus seats, too.

# The Boycott

The next day, Rosa met black church leaders at the Dexter Baptist Church. The minister was a young man named Martin Luther King.

There was silence when Rosa finished her story.

Then one man spoke. "Law's law," he said. "You must obey the law."

"Anyway, there's nothing we can do about it," said another.

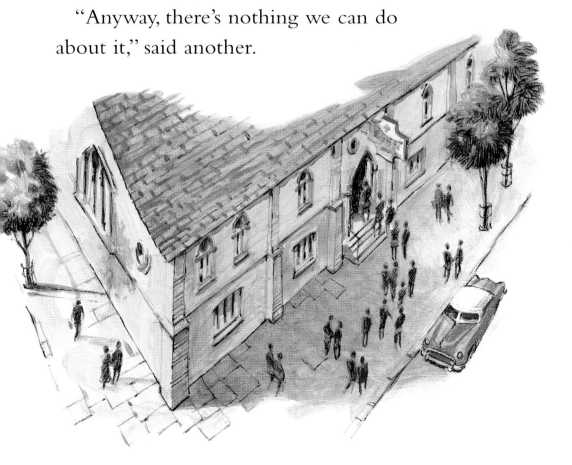

Suddenly, the young minister jumped up. "Oh, yes there is!" he said. "We can all stay off the buses. That way, the bus company will lose money. Then they'll have to treat us right."

Not everyone agreed. Many were scared of the white people.

"Oh, yeah, and get ourselves burned alive!"

"Or our homes bombed."

"What do you think, Rosa?" said the minister.

All eyes turned on her.

"I think it's time we stood up for our rights," she said quietly.

"Or sit in your case," someone said.

Everyone laughed. That broke the ice. It was agreed, and the call went out to all black people – DON'T RIDE THE BUSES.

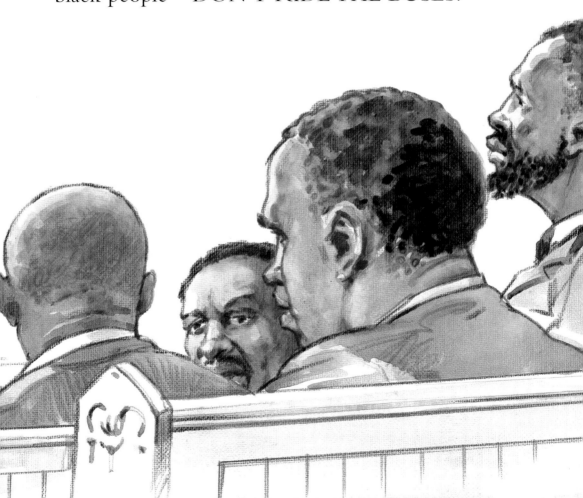

On Sunday night, the young minister walked slowly home. Martin was tired and worried.

Later, unable to sleep, he paced the floor, trying to comfort his two-week-old daughter. He thought about what he'd started.

What if it didn't work? Things would be worse than before – and white people would laugh at them.

The first bus of the day was due to pass his house at 6 A.M. But he couldn't bear to watch.

Then, suddenly, his wife Coretta called out, "Martin, Martin, come quickly!" He ran into the front room just as the bus went by.

It was empty!

Fifteen minutes later, the second bus was empty, too. And the third, and the fourth...

The early buses were usually packed
with black workers.

The boycott was working!

A year before Rosa Park's bus protest, the Supreme
Court had ruled that segregation in schools must end.
White and black children and students could go to the same
schools and colleges. The law also said that black people
could vote. But in the South, nothing changed, and white
people stopped black people from voting. Most black
people were too afraid to demand their rights.

# Love Your Enemy

That day, Martin and Rosa drove around town.
It was unbelievable – the streets were packed.

Men and women were walking as far as
ten miles to their downtown jobs. Students
were hitching rides to school. And an entire
family was riding a farm horse.

There wasn't a single black person waiting for a bus. Young black people stood on street corners, cheering and clapping the walkers and horse riders.

Outside City Hall, a jazz band was playing:

*Ain't gonna ride them buses no more.*
*Ain't gonna ride them buses no more.*
*Why in hell don't the white folks know*
*I ain't gonna ride them buses no more.*

The fight for black rights had begun.

That evening, Rosa went with Martin to a meeting. So many people turned up that the speeches had to be broadcast to them outside.

When Martin spoke, he was very nervous, looking around at Rosa for encouragement.

"We have to show white people we won't be kicked around any more," he said. "We should follow Rosa's example: protest with dignity. No violence. And another thing: we shouldn't hate our white brothers."

Some people shook their heads. A voice shouted, "How can you love someone who hates you?"

"It isn't easy," Martin said. "But we must always remember Jesus' words: 'Love your enemy.' In any case, if it comes to an open fight, the white people would win. They have the guns, the tanks, and the power."

But not all white people were racists. Some, especially in the north, wanted justice for all.

"We will make such a fuss, peacefully," said Martin finally, "that the whole world will get to know about us."

Rosa sat listening to Martin speak. She had never heard anyone like him. He seemed to express everyone's thoughts so clearly, inspiring everyone. When he sat down, there was a hush.

Then all through the church and streets
outside, people began to shout, clap, and sing.
They had found a leader.

While he was at college, Martin Luther King read
about the life of Mahatma Gandhi. The Indian leader
believed in non-violent protest and had led the people of
India against British rule. He told his people they must be
ready to go to jail, even die for freedom – but never kill for it.

Martin Luther King firmly believed that black people in the
United States should follow Gandhi's ideas.

# Montgomery Miracle

News of the "Montgomery Miracle" spread
across the country. Black people everywhere
began to follow the Montgomery example, and
a number of white people gave their support.

But other white people were angry. They
thought the world was laughing at them. In
desperation, they began a bombing campaign,
even blowing up Martin's house. Luckily, the
bomb went off on the porch. Baby Yoki was
sleeping at the back of the house; Coretta
was in the kitchen. They were unharmed.

This time Martin Luther King's family
had escaped. But would he and his followers
have the courage to fight on?

All over the south, black people guarded churches and houses, lighting them up at night.

One night, black people in Montgomery were woken by carloads of Ku Klux Klansmen rumbling through their district. The aim was clear: to scare black people into behaving "like niggers should."

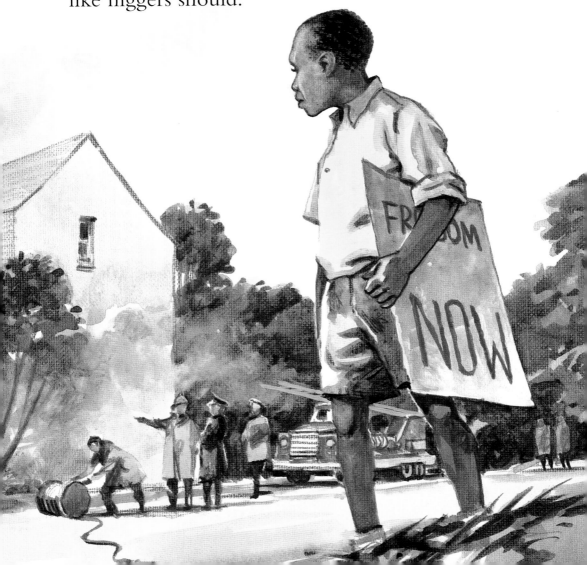

But this time black people stood up to them. Inspired by Martin, they didn't hide indoors and turn out the lights. Not this time! They switched on all the lights, opened their doors, and stood at the gates, waving and jeering.

The Ku Klux Klan were not used to being treated like a parade of circus clowns.

The black people appealed to the Supreme Court in faraway Washington to decide on their boycott of the buses.

To their surprise, the court said that bus segregation was against the law. Martin and his supporters had won!

The next day, Martin and Rosa got on a bus together.

The driver stopped Rosa. "Are you the Mrs. Parks who started the boycott?" he asked.

"Yes, I am."

"Welcome aboard, lady," he said with a smile. "Take any seat and have a nice day."

The three demands made by the bus boycotters were: that bus drivers should be polite to black people; that passengers should take their seats on a first-come, first-serve basis; and that there should be black drivers on routes that black people used most.

Until these demands were met, the black people of Montgomery stayed off the buses.

# Sit-ins

The Montgomery bus boycott was only the start. It inspired all sorts of protests throughout the south. One type of protest was the sit-in. One day, Martin went into a fast-food outlet with Yoki, who was now five years old.

"Burger and fries, please," he said politely. "And a banana milkshake for my girl."

People stared.

What was this black man doing in a whites-only restaurant? At first, the staff ignored him. Patiently, he kept repeating his order. Finally, the manager shouted, "Look, boy, we don't serve niggers. So, git!"

Martin said nothing. He just sat down at a table with Yoki. More black people entered, asking to be waited on.

Every day, they came back. Others did
the same in stores and libraries. No one
was waited on.

Stores began to lose money. The black
sit-ins scared white customers away. At the
end of the week, the manager of the fast-food
outlet came over to Martin.

"Here are your burger and fries, Sir," he said.
"And a banana milkshake, miss. Thank you
for your custom."

Slowly, but surely, other stores and restaurants throughout the southern states did the same. And in the parks, black people sat down on the whites-only benches. They came to realize an important truth: freedom is never given, it has to be won.

Not every campaign ended peacefully.
One evening, people were gathered in Martin's
church. All at once, bombs smashed through
the windows and a fire started. At first, it
looked like they would all burn to death.
But firemen arrived just in time to save them.

Others were not so lucky. When a bomb
exploded in a Baptist church in Birmingham,
Alabama, four young girls died, and 21 people
were badly hurt.

News of the actions by white mobs shocked the world.

One day, the phone rang in Martin Luther King's house.

"My name is John Kennedy," a voice said. "I'm running for President, and I want to help you."

The tide was turning. Things were starting to change.

After the 11 southern states lost the Civil War in 1865, white racists set up the Ku Klux Klan. This organization killed many hundreds of black people, often by burning them alive or hanging (lynching) them from trees. Many Klan members held important jobs, even in the police and the Mayor's office.

# We Shall Overcome

Though times were changing, there was one town still ruled by fear and hatred – Birmingham, Alabama. Here black people lived in fear of their lives. Libraries had even banned a book about black and white rabbits!

"If we can end segregation in Birmingham," Martin told his supporters, "we can stop it everywhere."

He was up against tough opposition.

Governor George Wallace and the police chief "Bull" Connor warned people, "The streets will run with blood if dirty niggers cause trouble."

It was Good Friday, a warm sunny day,
when Martin led a march down the main
street. A line of police blocked their path,
so the protesters linked hands, knelt, and sang
hymns. The police rushed in with clubs and
police dogs, taking hundreds off to jail. It
looked like the end of the Birmingham protest.

What happened next made history.

If grown-ups were afraid, children were not.
From all over town, a thousand black children,
some as young as six, came to join Martin.
They marched in twos, waving banners
and shouting, "Freedom now!"

When Bull Connor saw them,
he screamed, "Let those little niggers
have it! See those niggers run!"

People *did* see. Millions saw, all around the world. They watched the TV pictures with horror. Connor was laughing, and police were knocking children to the ground. Police dogs were snarling, and firemen were holding hoses. Children were crying and covered in blood.

So it went on, day after day. Then something odd happened. As usual, Connor ordered his men to attack. But this time, they didn't move.

"Damn it! Turn on the hoses!" he cried.

But, silently, the police and firemen turned aside – some had tears in their eyes. Martin's peaceful protest had won – thanks to the children.

Martin worked hard traveling up and down the country, telling the world about black people's problems. He went on some Freedom Rides when black people took buses from one state to another, sitting where they liked. That way, the protest movement spread. People began to realize that if they joined together to protest, they were strong.

The Freedom Rides, boycotts, and sit-ins hit the white racists where it hurt most – it made them lose money.

# Martin Escapes Death

By now, Martin had become leader of the American civil rights movement. "We're on the move," he said. "Like an idea whose time has come, not even mighty armies can stop us."

While he was in jail, Martin wrote his *Letter from a Birmingham Jail*. He was replying to an attack on him by eight white ministers. He explained what it was like to be black:

*When your last name is "nigger", your middle name "boy", your last name "John", when you're never Mr. or Mrs....*

The white ministers had told him to wait for rights to be given, to which he replied, "*Wait* nearly always means *never*."

Being in the public eye, Martin received hundreds of letters every day. Many were from black people thanking him and saying, "We are proud to have you as our leader."

But he also got sackfuls of hate mail from white racists. There were some people who wanted him dead.

One day, he was signing copies of his
book in New York when a woman came up.
"Are you Martin Luther King?" she asked.
"Why, yes, I am," he replied with a smile.
At that, the woman thrust a knife into his
chest. He was rushed to hospital where the
knife was removed. It had just missed his heart.

Martin went to jail many times, once for four months' hard labor. The racists did all they could to break him. But he battled on, believing that, "Freedom is never given to anybody. It has to be forced from the authorities."

During the summer of 1961, the Freedom Rides started to end bus segregation between states as well as in towns. The first freedom riders to reach Alabama were beaten up by the Ku Klux Klan, who set fire to their bus. People everywhere were shocked. The Supreme Court ruled that segregation on buses between was states illegal.

# I Have a Dream

In the summer of 1963, there was a civil rights
march from the Washington Monument to
the Lincoln Memorial in Washington. Nearly
a quarter of a million people came from all
over the country. There were poor black farm
workers from the south. There were famous
movie stars like Sidney Poitier and Marlon
Brando. There were as many white people as
black people, with black and white children
linking arms. It was the largest crowd in civil
rights history.

Martin was the last speaker. He had spent
hours planning his speech. Yet, as he stood
below the statue of Abraham Lincoln

and gazed at the sea of faces, he threw his notes aside and spoke from the heart.

"I have a dream," he cried, "of an Alabama where little black boys and black girls will be able to join hands with little white boys and white girls as sisters and brothers."

Swaying to and fro, people shouted, "Dream some more!"

He dreamed that freedom and justice would one day come to all America; that one day everyone would come together and sing the old freedom song: *Free at last. Free at last. Thank God Almighty, we're free at last!*

Martin gave the most moving speech people had ever heard. As they listened, tears streamed down their cheeks. Could the dream really come true?

In the White House afterward, President Kennedy shook Martin's hand and said, "That's my dream, too. You know, Martin, millions of white people have heard your message for the first time. We must fight racism together."

Martin added a word of warning.

"Remember, a hundred years ago, President Lincoln was shot for ending slavery."

The two men shook hands warmly. Whatever happened to them, they knew that one day their dream would come true.

Three months later, President Kennedy was shot dead while being driven with his wife through Dallas, Texas. Five years after that, in 1968, Martin was shot dead, too, on the balcony of his hotel room in Memphis, Tennessee. He was only 39. But his short life changed the lives of millions of African Americans.

On his gravestone are the words: "Free at last. Free at last. Thank God Almighty, I'm free at last."

# The Civil Rights Movement

The Civil Rights Act of 1875 claimed to give African Americans the same rights as white Americans, although many years would go by before all citizens really *were* equal.

By 1900, 18 states in the northern and western states had decided on various ways of tackling racial discrimination. Meanwhile, states in the south supported segregation laws.

During the next 55 years, there were many attempts to give blacks the same rights as whites, and some progress was made. It wasn't until Martin Luther King challenged the bus segregation laws in Montgomery that change really started to happen.

At last, in 1964, the Civil Rights Act, which banned discrimination, was passed by Congress. It was followed the next year by the Voting Rights Act. In a speech to Congress, President Lyndon Johnson, said that the act would "allow men and women to register and vote, whatever the color of their skin."

# Timeline

**1929** Jan 15     Martin Luther King born in Atlanta, Georgia.

**1954**     Martin becomes a minister in Montgomery, Alabama.

**1955** Dec     Rosa Parks arrested for taking a white bus seat. Martin leads the Montgomery bus boycott.

**1956** Feb 21     Martin jailed for the first time.

Nov 13     Supreme Court rules that bus segregation is illegal. Many states ignored the ruling for a time.

Dec 21     Montgomery buses desegregated. Sit-ins begin all over the south.

**1963** May 2     A thousand black children march through Birmingham.

Aug 28     Martin gives "I Have A Dream" speech in Washington.

**1964** Dec 10     Martin is the youngest person to receive the Nobel Peace Prize.

**1968** April 4     Martin shot dead in Memphis, Tennessee.

# More information

### Books to read
*Let the Trumpet Sound. A Life of Martin Luther King* by Stephen B. Oates, Canongate 1998.
*Martin Luther King, Jr* by Peter and Connie Roop, Heinemann 1998.
*Martin Luther King* by Valerie Schloredt and Pam Brown, Exley Publications 1988.
*I Have a Dream. The Story of Martin Luther King* by Neil Tonge, Hodder Wayland 2000.

### Websites
http://martinlutherking.8m.com/
http://www.seattletimes.com/mlk/

### Museum
The National Civil Rights Museum is in Memphis, Tennessee, on the site of Martin Luther King's assassination. Their website includes a virtual tour of the museum:
http://www.midsouth.rr.com/civilrights

# Glossary

**assassination** The killing of a well-known person.

**boycott** Refusing to use or buy certain goods or services.

**civil rights** A person's right to be free and equal with others.

**governor** The elected official in charge of a state.

**justice** When all is right and fair.

**Ku Klux Klan** A white secret society dedicated to keeping segregation.

**Lincoln, Abraham** President 1861-5, ended slavery after winning the Civil War; assassinated by a racist.

**nigger** An insulting name for a black person.

**racist** Someone who believes that one race is better than another.

**segregation** Keeping people apart.

**slave** A person owned by another.

**Supreme Court** The highest court in the United States.

# Index